Writing with POWER

Composition
Skills Practice

Perfection Learning®

© 2011 Perfection Learning® Corporation

The purchase of this book entitles an individual teacher to reproduce pages for use in the classroom. This permitted use of copyrighted material does not extend beyond the building level. Reproduction for use in an entire school system or for commercial use is prohibited. Beyond the classroom use by an individual teacher, reproduction, transmittal, or retrieval of this work is prohibited without written permission from the publisher.

Printed in the United States of America.

1 2 3 4 5 6 WC 16 15 14 13 12 11

For information, contact
Perfection Learning® Corporation
1000 North Second Avenue, P.O. Box 500
Logan, Iowa 51546-0500
Phone: 1-800-831-4190 • Fax: 1-800-543-2745
perfectionlearning.com

78006
ISBN-13: 978-0-7891-8013-1
ISBN-10: 0-7891-8013-8

Table of Contents

Chapter 1 A Community of Writers
Finding a Subject 1
Choosing and Limiting a Subject 2
Developing and Focusing a Subject 3
Classifying and Ordering Details 4
Drafting 5
Revising 6
Strategies for Editing 7

Chapter 2 Developing Style and Voice
Choosing Vivid Words; Figurative Language 8
Writing Concise Sentences 9
Creating Sentence Variety 10
Varying Sentence Beginnings 11
Correcting Faulty Sentences 12
Faulty Coordination 13–14
Rambling Sentences 15–17
Faulty Parallelism 18

Chapter 3 Structuring Writing
Topic Sentence 19
Supporting Sentences; Concluding Sentence 20
Features of a Good Paragraph 21
Introduction of a Composition 22

Chapter 4 Personal Writing
Drawing on Personal Experience 23
Developing and Selecting Details 24
Writing Narrative Paragraphs 25
Organizing Your Essay 26
Creating a Tone 27
Thesis Statement 28–30
Drafting and Revising 31–32

Chapter 5 Descriptive Writing
Specific Details and Sensory Words 33–35
Figurative Language 36
Identifying Your Audience 37
Writing Descriptive Paragraphs 38–39
Developing a Description 40–42
Organizing a Description 43

Table of Contents continued

Chapter 6 Creative Writing
Writing a Short Story 44
Writing a Short Story: Characters and Setting 45
Writing a Short Story: Drafting and Improving 46
Writing a Play: Characters and Setting 47
Writing a Play: Dialogue and Stage Directions 48
Writing a Poem 49
Writing a Poem: Sound Language and Figurative Language 50–51

Chapter 7 Expository Writing
Gathering Information 52
Organizing and Outlining 53
Writing Informative Paragraphs 54
Drafting the Thesis Statement 55
Drafting the Introduction 56
Body of a Composition 57
Conclusion of a Composition 58–59
Checking for Unity, Coherence, and Emphasis 60

Chapter 8 Writing to Persuade
Writing Persuasive Paragraphs 61
Facts and Opinion; Reasoning 62
Recognizing Propaganda 63
Choosing a Subject; Developing a Thesis Statement 64
Organizing an Argument 65

Chapter 9 Writing About Literature
Responding from Personal Experience 66
Responding from Literary Knowledge 67–68
Evaluating a Literary Work 69–70
Developing a Thesis; Evidence; Outlining 71
Drafting; Using Quotations; Revising 72

Chapter 10 Summaries and Abstracts
Recognizing Main Ideas 73
Condensing 74
Paraphrasing 75

Chapter 11 Research: Planning and Gathering Information
Evaluating Sources 76
Using the Library or Media Center 77
Using Print and Non-Print Reference Materials 78–79
Taking Notes and Summarizing 80

Chapter 12 Research: Synthesizing, Organizing, and Presenting
Writing a Working Thesis Statement; Organizing Notes 81–82
Outlining 83
Lists of Works Cited 84

Name _____ Date _____

CHAPTER 1 Finding a Subject

EXERCISE A Decide on a writing purpose that might be appropriate for developing each of the following limited subjects.

Example a word picture of my grandfather
to inform and entertain

1. a plea for a larger parking area at school

2. an article telling why the sea needs to be studied

3. a letter to the editor telling how I feel about billboards along roads

4. an essay explaining the differences between a reporter's job and columnist's job

5. an essay about the appearance of the buildings in a section of the downtown area

EXERCISE B On a separate sheet of paper, brainstorm a list of details you might include under one of the following subjects. Then decided on your purpose and your audience. To help you develop details, ask yourself *Where? What? When? Who? Why?* and *How?* about the subject.

1. shopping for the best buy
2. improving the appearance of my high school
3. describing an unusual friend or relative
4. telling how I manage my money
5. telling about an achievement I am proud of

EXERCISE C On a separate sheet of paper, develop a cluster on one of the following topics or one of your own. Include as many connections as you can.

- airports
- oceans
- agriculture
- automobiles
- personal heroes

Name _____ Date _____

CHAPTER 1   Choosing and Limiting a Subject

EXERCISE Use the topic you wrote about for Exercise C on page 1. Now use the following points to limit your subject.

1. Look in your prewriting for a subject that is of interest to you, that might be of interest to readers, and that you can cover thoroughly through your own knowledge. Write your subject below.
   _____

2. Limit your subject by focusing on a specific aspect or instance of it. Write your limited subject below.
   _____

3. Think about your limited subject and what you might like to say about it. What will be the purpose of your composition? Put a check beside your choice.

   _____ to explain or inform

   _____ to express your thoughts

   _____ to create

   _____ to persuade

4. Think about your subject and purpose. What audience are you most likely writing for? Answer these questions about your audience.

   a. Am I writing for children, teenagers, or adults?
   _____

   b. What does the audience already know about my subject?
   _____
   _____

   c. What words or terms might I need to define for the audience?
   _____
   _____

   d. Why will the audience be interested in my subject?
   _____
   _____

   e. What opinions will the audience have about my subject? How are these opinions like or unlike my own?
   _____
   _____

CHAPTER 1 Developing and Focusing a Subject

EXERCISE A Now you will develop the supporting details that will make your writing lively and interesting. Use all your senses, think about what you observe, and jot down your notes on this page. You may even want to make a sketch if you think that might help your writing. If you cannot observe your subject, try brainstorming. List all the details you can.

___

EXERCISE B Look over your supporting details and your other prewriting notes. What exactly do you want to say about your subject that interests you and suits your purpose and audience? Write your answer below.

CHAPTER 1 Classifying and Ordering Details

EXERCISE A Organize your material by thinking of categories into which you can put your supporting details. Try for at least three categories but not more than six. List each category below with the details that go with it.

_____

_____

_____

_____

_____

_____

_____

_____

_____

_____

EXERCISE B Check the type of order that makes the most sense for your material. Then number the categories you have listed above according to that order.

_____ chronological order

_____ developmental order

_____ spatial order

_____ logical order

_____ order of importance

_____ sequential order

CHAPTER 1 Drafting

> **EXERCISE A** Use the prewriting notes below to draft a paragraph for each topic on a separate sheet of paper. The first and last sentences are given.

1. **FIRST SENTENCE:**
   Online shopping has become a viable alternative to visiting malls and department stores.
   a. Web site photos and descriptions substitute for looking at items in person
   b. concerns about credit fraud addressed by encryption
   c. not maintaining stores and salespeople can mean lower prices
   d. time saved
   e. ease of arranging delivery or gift wrapping
   f. privacy and no holiday crowds
   g. can order items when regular stores are closed

   LAST SENTENCE:
   The Internet has brought with it a much higher level of consumer convenience.

2. **FIRST SENTENCE:**
   Our 50-year-old high school building is badly in need of renovation.
   a. heating system is the original
   b. heating is very noisy and unreliable
   c. air-conditioning system is nonexistent
   d. paint on hallway ceilings peeling
   e. windows let in cold air in winter
   f. window shades broken or missing entirely
   g. doors don't shut properly

   LAST SENTENCE:
   Any money spent on renovation will help raise the morale of those of us who spend part of our lives here.

> **EXERCISE B** Using your ideas from the exercises on pages 2–4, draft a paragraph on a separate sheet of paper. Save your draft for later use.

CHAPTER 1 Revising

EXERCISE A Read the following revised draft of a paragraph and then answer the following questions. Each sentence has been numbered.

(1) Skiing is one sport that lets you enjoy the beauty of winter and the colorful antics of other skiers. (2) Often everything at the top of the mountain is covered with a thin coat of ice. (3) On sunny days the whole top of the mountain looks like a fairyland. (4) The lift carries you up above the snow-covered slopes and graceful spruce trees. (5) Below, skiers are visible, *flashing through thick forests.* many of them zigzag in a graceful manner. but others seem stiff and awkward as they work their way slowly down the mountain. (6) All of them are dressed in colorful clothing. (7) ~~Ski clothing can be very expensive.~~ (8) The sun glinting on the ice and snow and the bright ski clothes all contribute to a beautiful scene.

1. Which sentence was out of order?

2. Which sentence was deleted because it strayed from the main idea?

3. Which rambling sentence was separated into three sentences?

4. Which sentence needed additional details?

EXERCISE B On a separate sheet of paper, revise the following paragraph. **(1)** Delete the sentence that strays from the main idea. **(2)** Add the transitions *for example* to one sentence and *even worse* to another. **(3)** Rewrite the final sentence to make it clearer and more interesting.

Driving defensively is a tactic every driver should learn. Defensive drivers learn to keep their attention on the road and on traffic conditions. Such drivers see every other car, every intersection, and every pedestrian as a possible hazard. The driver of a car ahead might stop suddenly or ignore a stop sign. A child or other pedestrian might cross the road without looking. Not every driver has learned the rules of defensive driving. This is why you should make defensive driving part of your driving habits. Young drivers are often more alert than older drivers. Many accidents can be prevented.

Name _____ Date _____

CHAPTER 1 Strategies for Editing

EXERCISE A Edit the following paragraphs for errors in grammar, spelling, usage, mechanics, and format. There are 10 errors in the first paragraph and 15 in the second.

Example Probably every one has has a diferent personal wish. Some times my presonal wish varies
Probably everyone has a different personal wish. Sometimes my personal wish varies.

1. If I had one personal wish it would be for a quite vacation with my family. My parents and my two brothers and me are all busy people. For instance, I may have band practice, and my younger brother may be at a soccor practice. My older brother may work late, also, my mother often attends one meeting or another and my father is often out of town for a few days. A quiet vacation would give us all a chance to do things together We'd have time to talk and laugh. A vacation together would give us a chance to become better aquainted.

2. When my friends learned that I was building a bat house they thought I was batty. They asked me if I did'nt know that bats are dangerous, That they swoop down on you and get entangled in you hair. This was my chance to tell them the truth about bats. Being the only flying Mammals bats are pretty wonderful. They eat up the flys and mosquitos that bother us. they pollenate the plants that produces fruit and flowers for us. They definately will stay away from our hair because they don't want to get caught in that mess on top of our heads. When you see a bat swooping in the air above you at twilight you know that you have a friend up their. My bat house will provide my little friends with a safe dry place to rest and sleep in.

EXERCISE B Revise and edit the paragraph you wrote for Exercise B on page 5. Then write a finished copy of your edited paragraph.

Name _____ Date _____

CHAPTER 2 Choosing Vivid Words; Figurative Language

EXERCISE A On the blank lines, write two specific words for each general word.

Example flower _____ *daisy, carnation* _____

1. speak _____
2. move _____
3. walk _____
4. large _____
5. pretty _____
6. run _____
7. lasting _____
8. quiet _____
9. think _____
10. aircraft _____

EXERCISE B Replace the underlined cliché in each sentence with new figurative language or specific image-creating words.

Example He was as mad <u>as a wet hen</u>. _____ *as a drenched cat* _____

1. Her room was as neat <u>as a pin</u>. _____
2. He's as hard <u>as nails</u>. _____
3. She's as happy <u>as a lark</u>. _____
4. I'm <u>as full as a tick</u>. _____
5. He's <u>a chip off the old block</u>. _____

CHAPTER 2 Writing Concise Sentences

EXERCISE A On the blank lines, write *R* if the sentence has unnecessary repetition. Write *EE* if the sentence contains an empty expression. Then underline the word or words that should be eliminated.

Example By 2:00 P.M. <u>in the afternoon</u>, the clouds had disappeared. R

1. Now and then I make trail mix every once in a while. _____
2. I think that I will photograph something for you with this new digital camera. _____
3. The thing is that my letter was lost in the mail. _____
4. We didn't get home on time because of the fact that we had a flat tire. _____
5. As a chorus member, Pete sang many solos by himself. _____
6. It seems as if everyone should learn first aid. _____
7. Jessica works at a job in the supermarket. _____
8. Your topic sentence seems too long in length. _____
9. The thing is that many dolphins swim along this shore. _____
10. It seems as if apparently no one read this article very carefully. _____

EXERCISE B On the blank lines, revise each sentence by shortening the underlined clause. You may rearrange words as long as you keep the original meaning.

Example Some Chinese ships have sails <u>that are square in shape</u>.
   Some Chinese ships have square sails.

1. In the ruins of ancient cities <u>that were built by the Mayas</u> are the remains of ball courts.
   _____

2. The Bay of Fundy is famous for its tides, <u>which are 40 feet high</u>.
   _____

3. Radios and clocks are manufactured from parts <u>that are mass-produced</u>.
   _____

4. Sanibel, <u>which is an island off the Florida coast</u>, is visited by many shell collectors.
   _____

5. A paddle <u>that is made for a canoe</u> is usually carved from spruce or white cedar.
   _____

Name _____ Date _____

CHAPTER 2 Creating Sentence Variety

EXERCISE A Combine each pair of sentences by using the method suggested in parentheses.

Example An artificial fountain is a stream of water. It is first raised by pressure. (adjective clause)
An artificial fountain is a stream of water that is first raised by pressure.

1. Natural fountains exist. They can be found in many parts of the world. (prepositional phrase)

2. People long ago copied natural fountains. They led water into a basin through pipes. (participial phrase)

3. Fountains were made of stone or bronze. They were made in the form of animals or people. (prepositional phrase)

4. The Fountain of Trevi is one example. It is an ancient Roman fountain. (appositive)

5. Many ancient fountains are preserved as works of art. Some modern ones are, too. (compound subject)

EXERCISE B Revise this paragraph so that it contains a mixture of simple, compound, complex, and compound-complex sentences. You may mark changes on this page. Then copy your final paragraph on a separate sheet of paper.

All countries have folk songs. People sing these songs at work, on special occasions, and at play. Europeans developed folk songs. Some of these men and women came to America. They brought their favorite tunes with them. Many old English ballads are still popular. The tunes remain the same. The words often change. For example, more than 100 versions of the ballad "Barbara Allen" have been collected. People of African ancestry provided some of America's greatest folk music. Many African Americans sang religious songs. They also made up work songs. Today modern singers make up songs. These songs sound like folk music. These songs are passed along and changed. Then some day they will become true folk songs.

CHAPTER 2 Varying Sentence Beginnings

EXERCISE A In each sentence, underline the construction or part of speech suggested in parentheses. Then reread the sentence, putting the underlined part at the beginning.

Example Annie Oakley was born in a log cabin <u>in 1866</u>. (prepositional phrase)

1. She practiced for long hours to become a perfect shot. (infinitive phrase)
2. She perfected her skills gradually. (adverb)
3. She had to use her rifle to help provide food for the family. (infinitive phrase)
4. She defeated Frank Butler at age 15 in a contest of marksmanship. (prepositional phrase)
5. Annie Oakley traveled with Buffalo Bill's troupe after she became famous. (adverb clause)
6. She became famous, performing before the crowned heads of Europe. (participial phrase)
7. Sitting Bull helped make her famous by giving her the title "Little Sure Shot." (prepositional phrase)
8. She fired 1,000 shots and broke 943 glass balls in one contest. (prepositional phrase)
9. She became famous eventually for hitting glass balls thrown in the air. (adverb)
10. Annie Oakley was immortalized in the musical *Annie Get Your Gun*. (prepositional phrase)

EXERCISE B Rewrite each sentence, varying the beginnings. As an opener, use the construction or part of speech suggested in parentheses.

1. A runner was hit with a thrown ball instead of being tagged when baseball was first played. (adverb clause)

2. You must have agility and talent to perform ballet dancing. (infinitive phrase)

3. Highland Scots wear traditional dress on special occasions. (prepositional phrase)

4. The Rocky Mountain goat, living among glaciers, blends into its background with its white coat. (participial phrase)

5. The penguins toddled eagerly to the edge of the pool. (adverb)

Name _____   Date _____

CHAPTER 2 Correcting Faulty Sentences

EXERCISE A On the blank line, write *faulty* if a sentence has faulty coordination or subordination. If a sentence is correct, write C.

Example __C__   Sally lost the set, and she still made the tennis team.

_____ 1. Bob saw a mouse, and he was looking under the bed.

_____ 2. Beverly likes sewing, so her friend has a new sewing machine.

_____ 3. The dog ate the bones, and he was a stray.

_____ 4. The plane took off, and the control tower hadn't given permission.

_____ 5. I like the story, but I think the ending is weak.

_____ 6. Working at summer camp is fun, and Jane is the swimming instructor.

_____ 7. Carl arrived very late; however, he couldn't find a seat.

_____ 8. Nancy burned the potatoes, and she was cooking supper.

_____ 9. Toni broke her pencil, and she was taking an examination.

_____ 10. Matt lost his watch, so he put an ad in the newspaper.

EXERCISE B Rewrite the following sentences, correcting faulty coordination or faulty subordination.

1. The squirrel bit open the acorn easily, and its teeth are very sharp.

   _____

2. I practice my dives every day, and Doug does a perfect swan dive.

   _____

3. I enjoyed the film, and I thought it was too scary.

   _____

4. Rob saw an accident, and he was crossing the road.

   _____

5. Dave often sits out much of a game; moreover, he is really a good halfback.

   _____

Name _____ Date _____

CHAPTER 2 — Faulty Coordination

EXERCISE Correct each sentence by using an appropriate coordinating word or phrase that shows the relationship between the two ideas.

1. Hannibal is considered the hometown of Mark Twain; besides, he was born in Florida, Missouri.
   _____
   _____

2. He was fascinated by the river; still, he became a river boat pilot.
   _____
   _____

3. During the Civil War, the river boats stopped running; moreover, Twain had to find a new job.
   _____
   _____

4. His brother was going to Nevada; on the other hand, Twain went with him.
   _____
   _____

5. Twain had experience as a reporter, yet he got a job with a newspaper.
   _____
   _____

6. He wrote many serious pieces; indeed, he soon became known for his humor.
   _____
   _____

7. He used much of his life in his writing, or his best-known work recalls his youth in Hannibal.
   _____
   _____

8. Twain created Tom Sawyer; instead, he created Huck Finn.
   _____
   _____

continued

Chapter 2: Faulty Coordination *continued*

9. Twain has brought laughter to millions; thus, he was not a happy man.
   _____
   _____

10. He was troubled by debts, so he was grieved by the deaths of his wife and daughters.
    _____
    _____

Name _____   Date _____

CHAPTER 2 Rambling Sentences

EXERCISE Revise each rambling sentence below by breaking it into shorter sentences. Add capital letters and punctuation marks where needed.

1. Our family goes blackberrying when the berries are ripe, and we have a routine that includes putting sulphur powder on our legs and insect repellent on our necks, and we take hooked sticks and large pails, and we wear sunglasses and wide-brimmed hats, and usually, because of our precautions, we manage to get home without bites, scratches, or sunstroke.

   _____
   _____
   _____
   _____

2. Trees shade us in summer and warm us in winter, and their wood has many uses, and although most trees are useful, a few can be dangerous, and one dangerous tree is called the *dynamite tree*, and it is native to Mexico, and this tree produces gourds with hard shells, about the size of oranges, and when the gourds mature, they explode, and bits of hard shell are hurled in all directions, and the sharp bits of shell sometimes hit bystanders and wound them.

   _____
   _____
   _____
   _____

3. The Spaniards under Ponce de León first came to Florida on Easter Sunday, 1513, and he named this land *Florida*, which means "flowery" in Spanish, and he may have done this because he saw so many beautiful flowers growing everywhere.

   _____
   _____
   _____
   _____
   _____

continued

Chapter 2: Rambling Sentences *continued*

4. Most of our nation's gold is stored in Fort Knox, where the storehouse is made of granite, concrete, and steel, and the door of the vault, which weighs more than 20 tons, has a number of separate combinations, and each is known only to a single individual, plus there are guards stationed all around, and an Army post is nearby.

   _____
   _____
   _____
   _____
   _____
   _____
   _____

5. You may be the kind of person who wakes up whistling and full of energy, or you may be the kind who doesn't wake up for several hours after getting out of bed, but the probability is that you are one or the other, for the world seems to be divided into day people and night people, and so which group you belong to may help determine where you work, how you relax, and even whom you marry.

   _____
   _____
   _____
   _____
   _____
   _____
   _____

continued

Chapter 2: Rambling Sentences continued

6. As closely as hurricanes are studied by meteorologists, they are still not fully understood, for while we know that they all begin as tropical storms, because hot air and warm seas provide the energy that powers the storm, no one really knows, however, why one tropical storm becomes a hurricane and another storm does not.

   _____

   _____

   _____

   _____

   _____

   _____

7. Computer programs can be copied with great ease, and as a result the protection of their products has become a critical issue for software developers, who are losing millions of dollars each year, and they are engaged, therefore, in an eager search for both electronic and legal means to protect the particular programs and approaches that they have developed.

   _____

   _____

   _____

   _____

   _____

   _____

Name _____ Date _____

CHAPTER 2 Faulty Parallelism

> **EXERCISE** Revise each sentence so that the grammatical constructions are parallel.

1. The woman's dark hair had loose curls and with blond streaks.
   _____

2. Lying on the beach, swimming, and an occasional run are my plans for the week.
   _____

3. Actually, to time a meal is often harder than cooking the food.
   _____

4. When Kenisha plays tennis, she swings accurately and with power.
   _____

5. As Howard tried to concentrate, he heard Savannah practicing the cello and a dog that barked at a cat.
   _____
   _____

6. Ari's hope was to find a steady job during the day, to paint in the evenings, and eventually that his paintings would sell.
   _____
   _____

7. The editorial was clear and strongly worded but without a point.
   _____

8. Please remember that the baby needs to be fed at one and to put him in his crib for a nap at two.
   _____
   _____

9. Becoming a test pilot is Kirby's dream, but to fulfill it will not be easy.
   _____

10. For her birthday my little sister received a toy frog that jumped, a big doll that talked, and a real yipping puppy.
    _____
    _____

CHAPTER 3 Topic Sentence

EXERCISE Underline the topic sentence in each of the following paragraphs.

1. When a friend graduates from high school, goes to the hospital, or celebrates a birthday, most of us send a card. <u>Sending greeting cards is one way we acknowledge important days.</u> Probably the earliest greeting cards were those sent on New Year's Day by the ancient Egyptians. Their custom was to send presents on that day, along with a written greeting. The early Romans also believed that January 1 was a day for gifts and greetings. Nowadays, printed cards are available for most holidays and special occasions. What started as a New Year's greeting has become a custom for greeting special days the year round.

2. <u>After their conquest of the Inca empire, the Spaniards found two magnificent, well-built, and parallel roads.</u> One, 24 feet wide, ran for 2,250 miles along the wild, mostly unsettled coast. The other scaled the heights of the Andes, sometimes in grades too steep for Spanish mules to climb. The Incas had designed their roads for sure-footed llamas and for seemingly untiring human runners. These strong runners had covered 1,200 miles in five to seven days, carrying the latest news from one end of the empire to the other. Parts of these roads still exist, and the Incas are still admired for their engineering skills.

3. A typical automobile today has more than 5,000 parts. <u>The raw materials for automobile parts come from every corner of the world.</u> The shiny chrome used for decorations comes from ore mined in Africa and Turkey. Cork from trees in Portugal is used for making gaskets that do not leak. Seat cushions are made from the fibers of the jute plant grown in Southeast Asia. The rubber for tires is grown in Asia and Africa. Of course, many other materials, such as glass and iron, are found right here in the United States. An American-made car is a prime example of international trade agreements.

4. <u>Weather experts use many tools in trying to gather information and predict weather patterns.</u> One of these tools is the weather balloon. Huge plastic balloons circle the earth collecting weather information. These balloons carry scientific instruments that measure the winds, temperature, pressure, and humidity. They relay these measurements to the ground by radio. This information is then examined carefully and issued to predict changes in weather patterns across the nation. The balloons fly as high as 50,000 feet and can circle the earth many times before wearing out and dropping to Earth.

Name _____ Date _____

CHAPTER 3 Supporting Sentences; Concluding Sentence

EXERCISE A After each topic sentence, write the letters of the sentences below that support it. A detail may support more than one topic sentence.

TOPIC SENTENCE 1: Fungi are all around us.
TOPIC SENTENCE 2: Fungi are unusual kinds of plants.
TOPIC SENTENCE 3: Fungi can both help and harm us.

   A. You have probably seen fungi growing on trees or decaying logs.
   B. Unlike most plants, fungi do not have leaves, flowers, roots, or stems.
   C. Penicillin, which comes from a mold fungus, saves many lives.
   D. Slime molds, which are usually regarded as fungi, often show characteristics of lower forms of animal life.
   E. The yeast that the baker uses to make bread light and fluffy is a fungus.
   F. Fungi lack chlorophyll, which enables other plants to make their own food from sunlight.
   G. Some mushrooms, usually ones with umbrella-shaped caps, are good to eat.
   H. Fungi have to feed on other plants or animals.
   I. Mushrooms are another common kind of fungus.
   J. Since some mushrooms are very poisonous, you should never eat any kind you find growing wild.
   K. Invisible fungi in the air produce the mildew that grows in hot, humid weather.
   L. Many people have found harmful fungi living on their feet.

EXERCISE B Write two possible concluding sentences for the paragraph below.

   High technology has come up with a labor-saving device for tracking wild animals. To study the life habits of an animal, scientists tranquilize it and put on a collar to which a radio transmitter has been attached. The device sends out beeps, enabling the scientists to keep track of the animal's whereabouts, although recapturing the animal can be difficult. Now a device has been invented that anesthetizes the animal by remote control. A special collar includes two drug-filled dart assemblies that can be activated by radio. Once an animal is found, the scientist presses a button. The darts in the collar release the drug into the animal and tranquilize it for its checkup.

_____
_____
_____
_____

Name _____ Date _____

CHAPTER 3 Features of a Good Paragraph

EXERCISE A Find the topic sentence. Then cross out sentences that stray from the main idea. Add the following specific details to the paragraph. Use a separate sheet of paper for your work.

> 16 peaks
> peaks more than 6,000 feet high
> 40 percent of park has virgin forest
> more than 1,000 plant species
> types of animals: bears, foxes, raccoons, bobcats, wild turkeys

> The Great Smoky Mountain National Park is noted for its rich variety of plants and animals and for its peaks that rise above sea level. Many native tree species can be found here. Motorists use its main highway to go from Tennessee to North Carolina. Some of the park is covered with virgin forest. Many plant species grow here. The park was dedicated on September 2, 1940. As a wildlife sanctuary, it is the home of many animals. A visit to this park can give you an idea of what America was like before the settlers came.

EXERCISE B As you read the following paragraph, identify each numbered connective by writing *repeated key word*, *synonym*, *pronoun*, or *transition* on the blank lines.

> Going on a nature trail walk can be a fascinating experience. Last Saturday our leader, Joe, who was the **(1)** guide on this walk, got all ten of us to quit talking while **(2)** he gave us his lecture about not stepping on any wildflowers. **(3)** Then we started off. **(4)** In a while we came to a stream. **(5)** He pointed out a bed of bluets near some buttercups and explained why this was a good place for such **(6)** wildflowers to grow. **(7)** Next, he stopped in the woods to show us a rare flower, a **(8)** yellow ladyslipper. It was growing right next to a jack-in-the-pulpit. **(9)** Finally, we came to the end of the trail. We had seen thirty or forty **(10)** wildflowers and listened to Joe's description of each one.

1. _____
2. _____
3. _____
4. _____
5. _____

6. _____
7. _____
8. _____
9. _____
10. _____

Name _____ Date _____

CHAPTER 3 • Introduction of a Composition

EXERCISE Read the following composition introductions. First, underline the sentence in the paragraph that acts as the thesis statement. Then answer the questions that follow each introduction.

1. When patrons entered the colorful gates, they were greeted by two mechanical clowns, swaying and giggling in unison. Tinkling calliope music drifted through the air, and the shining lights from the miniature Ferris wheel and twenty-horse carousel beckoned to everyone. Although I was only five at the time, I will remember my time there forever. <u>The recently demolished Candyland Amusement Park was an essential and enjoyable attraction for Marionville's children, and it will be sorely missed.</u>

   a. Is the tone of this introduction amusing, angry, or nostalgic?

   _____

   b. Does the writer capture the reader's attention through statistical facts or informative details?

   _____

2. My older sister Rachel recently applied for a job at a leading publishing company. Although her high school transcripts were impressive, and her references from past jobs were all excellent, she did not land the job. The reason? Her typing and office skills were not on par with other applicants. Now Rachel wishes she had been required to take typing/keyboarding classes at Roosevelt High School. <u>I believe we should stop future Roosevelt graduates from encountering the problem Rachel has faced; we should demand that the school board make typing/keyboarding classes not an option but a requirement.</u>

   a. Is the tone of this introduction serious, joyful, or angry?

   _____

   b. Is the main purpose to inform, to express, or to persuade?

   _____

3. <u>Perhaps the most entertaining mixture of sports and comedy in the 1970s could be found with the Harlem Globetrotters.</u> Led by such stars as Meadowlark Lemon and Curly Neal, the Globetrotters displayed their amazing basketball-playing abilities, astonishing trickery, and witty banter to audiences around the world.

   a. Is the tone of this introduction straightforward, argumentative, or sad?

   _____

   b. Is the main purpose to persuade or to explain/inform?

   _____

CHAPTER 4 Drawing on Personal Experience

EXERCISE A From your personal experience, list three possible subjects for a personal essay. The following are possible sources of ideas.

    favorite possessions   family activities
    favorite places   interaction with friends or strangers
    favorite activities   childhood learning experiences

1. _____
2. _____
3. _____

EXERCISE B Choose the subject above that is most significant to you. Write it on the line below. Then answer the following questions.

SUBJECT: _____

1. What do you remember most about the experience?
   _____
   _____

2. How did the experience affect you at the time?
   _____
   _____

3. Why is the experience important to you now?
   _____
   _____

EXERCISE C In a sentence or two based on your answers to the questions in Exercise B, explain how the experience could be meaningful to your audience.

_____
_____
_____

Name _____ Date _____

CHAPTER 4 Developing and Selecting Details

> **EXERCISE** Brainstorm details for your personal essay by writing specific details under the following headings. Use additional paper, if necessary.

1. **EVENTS** (Write down details, using your five senses.)

   _____
   _____
   _____
   _____
   _____

2. **PEOPLE** (Visualize each person you are writing about, starting at the head and slowly moving down to the feet.)

   _____
   _____
   _____
   _____
   _____

3. **PLACES** (Start at one side of the setting and visualize slowly to the other side.)

   _____
   _____
   _____
   _____
   _____

4. **FEELINGS** (Focus on your feelings and reflections as you move through the experience.)

   _____
   _____
   _____
   _____
   _____

Name	Date

CHAPTER 4 Writing Narrative Paragraphs

EXERCISE A The topic sentence and concluding sentence of a paragraph are identified below. On the blank lines, number the details in chronological order.

TOPIC SENTENCE

My family and I started off on a month's camping tour of the Midwest.

_____ She built the nest of mud and twigs and then laid three eggs in it.

_____ We spotted a robin building a nest on top of our fuel tank.

_____ Between hikes, swims, and cookouts, we watched as the eggs hatched and the fledglings grew and finally flew off.

_____ She settled on her eggs as we stood by helplessly.

_____ We never got beyond our first stop, a state park in Illinois.

_____ Since state law forbids the disturbance of nesting birds on state property, we were stuck right there.

CONCLUDING SENTENCE:

We decided that watching the robin family grow had been the best part of our one-stop tour.

EXERCISE B On a separate sheet of paper, write the paragraph above. Add transitions where needed to show how the events are related in time, and add other extra words if necessary.

EXERCISE C Indicate the point of view in each sentence by writing *first person* or *third person* on the blank line.

Example During a lull in the storm, Peter dashed out to the dock.   _third person_

1. Last winter, in an idle moment, I signed up for a course in scuba diving.   _____

2. Tim screwed up his courage and walked purposefully over to where Sarah sat quietly in one corner.   _____

3. Paula came to a full stop at the crossroads and studied her road map carefully.   _____

4. When I first saw the whale surface near our boat, I couldn't believe my eyes.   _____

5. Ever since I was in the first grade, I have had a deadly fear of snakes.   _____

CHAPTER 4 Organizing Your Essay

EXERCISE A Read each of the following introductory paragraphs and decide how you would develop each essay by writing *chronological, spatial, importance,* or *developmental* on the blank line.

_____ 1. There are many incredible things about going to Camp Huarachi. The price of the camp during summer, for one thing, is relatively inexpensive. Even more important than that are all the skills, crafts, and hobbies you learn. But above everything else I value about the camp are all the terrific friendships I inevitably make each summer.

_____ 2. Mrs. McCormick was a nervous but skilled substitute teacher. When she first walked into our room, we looked at each other gleefully, suspecting she would would prove too timid to give us homework. But we were wrong. She told us to open our books to page 236. Next, she gripped the chalk in her hand with firm authority and began to write assignments on the board. Finally, she cleared her throat and told us, "Quiet down."

_____ 3. Pleasantville is a sleepy but beautiful little town, just down the road from McPherson. At the far north of town are two large grain elevators. In the center of town, a small city park, well groomed and always packed with happy children, is an obvious highlight. And to the south of town, close to its grocery store and hamburger joint, is the world-famous Pleasantville attraction, the world's largest rubber ball.

EXERCISE B Find an article from a newspaper or magazine. Search the article to find examples of paragraphs that use different types of organization: developmental, chronological, spatial, and order of importance.

CHAPTER 4 Creating a Tone

EXERCISE Read each of the following essay introductions and decide on the writer's tone. Then write on the blank line *reflective, sad, suspenseful,* or *humorous.*

_____ 1. My friend Tony may look like an ordinary guy, but if you hang around him long enough, you discover that he has two left feet and two hands that have never met, let alone learned to communicate with each other. Everything he touches seems to drop and break or disappear altogether from the face of the earth. For every three rungs on a ladder he climbs, he manages to fall back two. His friends have learned to grab Tony's arms and hold tight whenever he approaches a rug. Otherwise, talented Tony would somehow catch his toe on the rug's edge and end up sprawled across the room.

_____ 2. For all his faults, my friend Tony does possess one trait that makes him appealing to everyone he meets. Tony can see the humor in almost every event. Not only does he see the funny side, but also he has a talent for infecting those around him with his sense of humor. Being able to laugh at himself is an especially wonderful asset of his.

_____ 3. When Tony and I first saw the roller coaster at Hampton Park, we egged each other on to try a ride. As we settled in the front seats, we joked and laughed. The ride up to the top of the first rise was slow and easy. We had time to look around and wave at the people below. Then it happened. I screamed and gripped the bar in front of me as we circled down and around, going faster and faster. In his panic Tony let go of the bar altogether and threw his hands in the air. He seemed to rise up out of his seat and lean dangerously toward the outside of the car. I wanted desperately to grab him and shove him down deeper in his seat, but my hands seemed glued to the bar in front of me. A ride that had started as a lark now seemed a battle for survival.

Name _____ Date _____

CHAPTER 4 Thesis Statement

EXERCISE A On a separate sheet of paper, make a list of possible subjects by answering the following questions. Then brainstorm for ideas that could provide a clear and powerful thesis statement for the subject. Write your possible thesis statement on the blank lines provided.

1. What town or city have I seen that has particularly impressed me?
   _____
   _____

2. Who is one person from my childhood who had a strong influence on me?
   _____
   _____

3. What event from my high school years has helped me make decisions about my future?
   _____
   _____

4. What news item have I recently learned or heard about that I could explain briefly to others?
   _____
   _____

5. What piece of music means the most to me?
   _____
   _____

EXERCISE B Using the brainstorming notes you wrote for Exercise A, write a rough draft of your introduction. Be sure to include a thesis statement to state your main idea and make your purpose clear.

_____
_____
_____
_____
_____
_____

continued

Chapter 4: Thesis Statement *continued*

EXERCISE C Read the following introductory paragraphs. Then identify each thesis statement by underlining it.

1. My mother gave me one of her greatest gifts when she taught me to make a quilt. I remember that winter; I had broken my ankle while skating on Lake Raymond and was forced to spend the days inside the house. My mother noticed how disappointed I was. One day, she stepped into my room with a smile on her face, holding a sewing kit and a paper bag filled with scraps of cloth. Little did I know what was about to happen.

2. If you are frightened by cemeteries, you aren't alone; some of our ancestors were too. The early writings of American settlers show many fascinating, incredible, and sometimes funny superstitions associated with funerals, mausoleums, and cemeteries. For instance, did you know it was believed pointing at a hearse would mean a loved one would soon pass away? Or that it was bad luck to whistle in a graveyard? It was considered bad luck, too, to read too many names on gravestones or to walk over a grave. These are only a few of the superstitions some of our ancestors believed.

3. In today's media much emphasis is put on the longing to avoid the signs of aging. We see television commercials touting anti-aging creams, magazines ads for supposedly helpful supplements, and even subway posters for plastic surgeons. It is obvious, however, that the most simple and important methods for staying and feeling young lie in the areas of exercise and diet.

EXERCISE D Write a thesis statement based on the ideas and information provided below.

1. **SUBJECT:** candlepin bowling

   DETAILS:
   - has many differences from regular bowling: ball is smaller, pins are taller, and scoring is different
   - still played frequently in the New England states, but not as popular as regular bowling
   - takes a while to become accustomed to differences, and many think candlepin is more difficult
   - after playing it several times, I actually enjoy it more

   THESIS STATEMENT:

   _____

   _____

continued

Chapter 4: Thesis Statement continued

2. **SUBJECT:** the attractions and drawbacks of joining the school band

   DETAILS: • the joy of learning to read music and to play an instrument
   • the sense of camaraderie with other school musicians
   • the fun extracurricular parades and music festivals
   • the possibility of spending more time practicing and less on school studies

   THESIS STATEMENT:
   _____
   _____

Name _____ Date _____

CHAPTER 4 Drafting and Revising

EXERCISE A Revise the following paragraph by adding specific details that would help the readers better visualize or understand the experience.

> As Tony and I stood on the deck of the ferry crossing the sound, the weather turned bad. After a few minutes of trying to keep my balance, I glanced at Tony. He looked very peculiar. He looked just about the way I was beginning to feel. Neither of us was a good sailor, and the condition of the water surrounding us gave both of us a scare. As we staggered toward a bench out of the wind, Tony uttered some strange sounds. It sound to me as if he'd better go inside and lie down.

_____
_____
_____
_____
_____
_____
_____

EXERCISE B Revise the tone of the following paragraph by replacing any formal, technical, or unfamiliar words with more familiar, everyday vocabulary that sounds more natural.

> Neither of us was able to ingest the repast we had procured at the snack bar on the ferry. Just the sensory perception of food was too much for our stomachs to absorb. Most of the passengers sitting near us looked as nauseated as we felt. I'm sure we were all wondering if we would ever arrive at our port of call in one piece or whether we would have to use the lifeboats and endeavor to survive on the open sea. The thought was not exactly a happy one. We sat there in utter misery for over an hour before the ferry finally pulled into its slip at the harbor.

_____
_____
_____
_____
_____
_____

continued

Name   Date

Chapter 4: Drafting and Revising *continued*

> **EXERCISE C** Return to the details you wrote for preparing a personal essay on page 24. Then prepare a draft of the complete essay. Prepare a final copy, revising the draft carefully for tone, sensory details, and appropriate wording.

Name _____ Date _____

CHAPTER 5 Specific Details and Sensory Words

EXERCISE A Rewrite the following sentences, replacing the underlined sections with more specific details or sensory words.

Example At the circus, Beulah saw a strange sight.
At the circus, Beulah saw three clowns riding a mule that wore pink pajamas.

1. The attractive female tiptoed across the floor.
   _____

2. William Faulkner was a really good writer.
   _____

3. Ricco cooked an interesting dish for dinner yesterday.
   _____

4. Central Park has some neat features.
   _____

5. Kathy wore some really strange clothes at the picnic last week.
   _____

6. He was born on a certain day of the week that had odd weather.
   _____

7. That interesting-looking jockey rode that type of horse through the town's streets.
   _____
   _____

8. Mrs. Schwartz has a kind personality and always treats us to chocolate bars.
   _____
   _____

9. For my report I read that famous book by that author.
   _____
   _____

continued

Name _____   Date _____

Chapter 5: Specific Details and Sensory Words *continued*

10. Why does your kitchen <u>have that intriguing smell</u>?
    _____
    _____

11. <u>A certain player from a certain sports team</u> hungrily ordered two pepperoni pizzas.
    _____
    _____

12. To me, the music of the Country All-Stars sounds <u>not all that great</u>.
    _____
    _____

EXERCISE B Read the following four groups of words. Then write two specific examples each of sight, sound, smell, taste, or touch that can describe each item. Be as detailed and evocative as possible in your list of sensory details.

Example a trip to the zoo

Sight the dark, blue-lit caves of the bat exhibit; the towering giraffes shading themselves beside the weeping willow trees

Sound the siren calls of an exotic bird; frightened children crying in the reptile room

Smell the sludgy, stagnant water in the elephant cage; a mixture of peanuts and popcorn at the refreshment stand

Taste the sugary cotton candy; the salty peanuts we eat instead of giving them to the elephants

Touch the cold, rough bars of the barriers; the leathery feel of a snake I'm allowed to hold

1. the worst meal in your school cafeteria

   Sight _____

   Sound _____

   Smell _____

   Taste _____

   Touch _____

continued

Name _____   Date _____

Chapter 5: Specific Details and Sensory Words *continued*

2. the coldest morning you remember

   Sight _____

   Sound _____

   Smell _____

   Taste _____

   Touch _____

3. a busy weekend in a big city

   Sight _____

   Sound _____

   Smell _____

   Taste _____

   Touch _____

4. the crowd at a sporting event

   Sight _____

   Sound _____

   Smell _____

   Taste _____

   Touch _____

Name _____ Date _____

CHAPTER 5 Figurative Language

EXERCISE Read the following sentences. Then rewrite them, using the type of figurative language in parentheses to add depth and color to each.

Example Julia swam across the lake. (simile)
Julia swam across the lake as effortlessly as a dolphin.

1. When I walked into the room, many people watched me. (hyperbole)

2. The sun rose above the hills. (metaphor)

3. Billy's haircut is strange. (simile)

4. My little sister did the dishes. (metaphor)

5. When I heard the explosion, I felt fear. (personification)

6. She felt the blades of grass on her legs. (simile)

7. Not many people love ice cream as much as Gina. (hyperbole)

8. The rain fell on my father's soybean crop. (personification)

9. My tongue felt fuzzy in my mouth. (metaphor)

10. The llama strutted around the yard. (simile)

Name _____   Date _____

CHAPTER 5 — Identifying Your Audience

EXERCISE A Identify three different possible audiences for each of the following descriptive subjects.

Example the Milky Way
an astronomer; an astronaut; a student writing a paper on the solar system

1. a certain fashion designer
   _____
   _____

2. famous people from your home state
   _____
   _____

3. Palomino horses
   _____
   _____

4. a director of comedy films
   _____
   _____

5. Vietnamese cooking
   _____
   _____

6. volleyball
   _____
   _____

EXERCISE B Choose one of the six topics from the previous exercise. On a separate sheet of paper, write a descriptive paragraph, using specific details and figurative language. Keep in mind the analysis of your possible audience for the material. When you have finished, read the paragraph to the rest of your class, and discuss how the paragraph limits or specifies an audience.

Name _____ Date _____

CHAPTER 5 Writing Descriptive Paragraphs

EXERCISE A For each subject, list three sensory details you could use in developing a descriptive paragraph.

Example basement workshop

smell of wood chips, the smooth feel of fine-grained boards, loud buzzing of a sanding machine

1. bus station

2. gymnasium

3. hardware store

4. kitchen at home

5. a city park

continued

Chapter 5: Writing Descriptive Paragraphs *continued*

EXERCISE B Underline all of the transitional words or phrases in the following paragraph. On the blank line, indicate the type of spatial order used to develop the paragraph.

Nothing of the man huddled on the bleachers showed except his clothes. On top of his head was a red woolen ski cap pulled over his ears and folded back just over his eyebrows. Below that, a huge orange and black muffler circled his neck, obscuring his face. Lower, his heavy pile coat, with its collar turned up, hung to his feet. Underneath the hem of his all-enveloping coat, the toes of his rubber boots just peeped out. I left the stadium never glimpsing the man wrapped up inside. This time the clothes really did make the man.

_____

EXERCISE C Using one set of sensory details you wrote in Exercise A, write a descriptive paragraph on a separate sheet of paper.

Name _____ Date _____

CHAPTER 5 Developing a Description

> **EXERCISE A** With an overall impression in mind and a vision of your audience, you can now use strategies for developing your description. Read the following list of details for specific descriptions. Then choose the two items that would not fit with the rest of the description and underline them. On the blank lines that follow, explain why these items would not fit.

1. **OVERALL IMPRESSION:** The Thimbles, a new band you like, and their two smash hits on the radio

   DETAILS: a band you liked last year that no one else seemed to follow; The Thimble's first hit, "My One and Only"; their second hit, "Silver Sunshine"; The Thimble's lead singer, Mauricio Mason; the upcoming full-length CD by the band, as-yet untitled; a book currently in bookstores that has a chapter on bands you like

   _____
   _____

2. **OVERALL IMPRESSION:** the allure of Cape Cod, Massachusetts, in the summertime

   DETAILS: the Cape Cod city of Hyannis and all its summer festivities; the cranberry harvesting in late autumn; the summer activities in nearby Providence, Rhode Island; the exciting beachfront city of Provincetown, at the tip of Cape Cod; the number of tourists who visit Cape Cod each summer; the joy of fishing and whale watching during the summer in Cape Cod

   _____
   _____

3. **OVERALL IMPRESSION:** a quiet evening at home, watching television with friends

   DETAILS: your friend Martha makes peppermint tea for all of you; you put some logs in the fireplace and listen to the soft crackling of the fire; your friend Tim turns up the TV volume as a gang of thieves loudly makes a bank heist; you watch a ballet on the public television station with the sound turned down; the following day, you all have to go back to work; three of your friends fall asleep in front of the fire

   _____
   _____

4. **OVERALL IMPRESSION:** a barn filled with horses on a warm, peaceful day

   DETAILS: the meteorologist on the radio predicts thunderstorms for the evening; two quarter horses softly nuzzle each other's noses under the shade of the barn roof; the warm breeze filters the fragrant smell of hay and alfalfa; barn swallows twitter in the eaves above the horses; in the neighbor's barn, a newborn calf makes a terribly loud noise; the horseman's young son enters the barn and softly uses a curry comb on his favorite horse

   _____
   _____

continued

Name _____ Date _____

Chapter 5: Developing a Description *continued*

> **EXERCISE B** Choose one of the overall impressions you wrote about in Exercse A. Now freewrite to think of details of your own that would describe that impression. Using a separate sheet of paper, write a descriptive paragraph, filtering details to choose those most pertinent and vivid for your impression.

> **EXERCISE C** Read the following objective sentences. Then rewrite the sentences, adding details that change the objective stance to subjective. Be sure your reader will be able to discern your opinion about the subject.

Example Mice live in our house.
The mice in our house are stupid, because they keep getting caught in our traps.

1. Amanda went to Brazil.

2. You are listening to a CD.

3. The snow is falling.

4. Have you taken your bath?

5. Waleed is wearing new shoes.

6. The dog is barking.

continued

Name _____ Date _____

Chapter 5: Developing a Description *continued*

EXERCISE D Using what you have learned about analyzing an audience, developing a description, and filtering details, write two paragraphs about one of the following subjects. For the first paragraph, write your description to make it negative, directed toward an audience who also feels negatively about the subject. For the second paragraph, use the same topic, but try a positive description, directing it toward an audience who feels positively about the subject.

POSSIBLE SUBJECTS:
- the new mall in your town
- a new movie playing this weekend
- a particular brand of shoes
- a fast-food restaurant
- basketball
- the length of summer vacation
- a type of candy bar
- public transportation

Name _____   Date _____

CHAPTER 5 — Organizing a Description

> **EXERCISE A** For the following sentences, identify what type of order is being used for the description. On the blank lines provided, write *SP* for spatial, *C* for chronological, *SQ* for sequential, *OI* for order of importance, or *D* for developmental.

Example _D_ When Gabriel remembered the days he spent at summer camp, he thought about the flavorless gruel they served for breakfast, the boring bunk mate who wouldn't speak to him, and the tiny bluebird that sang to him every night from the window of his cabin.

_____ 1. My brother John ran from the room, tipped over a chair, turned around to see our reaction, and disappeared down the hall.

_____ 2. In order to make a banana split, you must first cut a banana in half, then scoop three helpings of ice cream between the halves, and finally drizzle the scoops with chocolate syrup, whipped cream, and chopped nuts.

_____ 3. When we walked into the kitchen, we saw the spoons and forks dumped onto the floor at the left, the plates broken in the center of the floor, and Tammy's prize vase shattered at the right.

_____ 4. The most important reason for vacationing in Beachville is to have your spirits brightened by the wonderful weather; additional reasons are to relax on the beach, to hear the wonderful Beachville music, and finally to meet the Beachville citizens.

> **EXERCISE B** Read the following list of items on the subject of painting your room. Then use a separate sheet of paper to write a paragraph that organizes each detail into a logical and meaningful description. Add at least five details of your own to the details you have been given, and be sure to include examples of at least two of the types of figurative language you have learned: simile, metaphor, personification, and hyperbole.

- after lunch, the painting seems to go more smoothly
- you and Robert return home and head for your room
- at dinner, Robert notices the restaurant is painted in "sweet cream" paint
- Robert at last heeds your advice and slows down
- you are almost finished when your father gets home in the afternoon
- you and Robert go to the hardware store to buy paint
- you begin to paint the walls
- you clear the room of furniture and put newspaper on the floors
- your cat rushes into the room and spills some paint
- Robert paints faster than you do, and you begin to argue with him
- at lunchtime, your mother makes grilled cheese sandwiches
- your friend Robert arrives at your house, dressed in his painting outfit
- your father is so pleased with your room, he takes you out for dinner
- the store assistant helps you select "sweet cream" paint

CHAPTER 6 Writing a Short Story

EXERCISE A Complete this plan for a narrative by writing a conflict and creating a possible resolution or outcome.

NARRATOR/POINT OF VIEW: Third-person omniscient

SETTING: Deep in the woods, late at night

CHARACTERS AND BRIEF DESCRIPTIONS: Steve, a camp counselor, and his three 16-year-old camp helpers: Donna, Maria, and David

EVENT TRIGGERING ACTION: The four have become lost in the woods and begin hearing noises in the distance

CONFLICT: _____
_____
_____
_____
_____
_____

STRUGGLE TO RESOLVE CONFLICT: _____
_____
_____
_____
_____
_____
_____

OUTCOME: _____
_____
_____
_____
_____
_____

EXERCISE B On a separate sheet of paper, create a plan for a story of your own.

Name _____ Date _____

CHAPTER 6 Writing a Short Story: Characters and Setting

EXERCISE A Write a description of a character for your story. First, complete the following sentences. Then, on a separate sheet of paper, write a paragraph describing your character.

1. The character's name is _____

2. His/Her age is _____

3. His/Her eyes are _____

4. His/Her hair is _____

5. His/Her voice is _____

6. His/Her general size is _____

7. His/Her physical condition is _____

8. His/Her typical mannerisms are _____

9. His/Her background is _____

10. His/Her personality traits are _____

EXERCISE B Plan the setting for your story. Include answers to the following questions.

1. Is the setting urban, or is it rural? _____

2. What season of the year is it? _____

3. What time of day is it? _____

4. What is the weather like? _____

5. Where does the action occur, indoors or outdoors? _____

6. If indoors, what kind of room or building? _____

7. If outdoors, what is the terrain? _____

8. What significant objects are visible? _____

9. What mood are you trying to create? _____

10. What special conditions foretell coming events? _____

Name _____ Date _____

CHAPTER 6 — Writing a Short Story: Drafting and Improving

EXERCISE A Before writing a draft of your story, follow the guidelines below.

1. On the line below, identify which story idea you have chosen.
   _____

2. Choose the type of conflict your main character will face. On the line below, write *conflict with self, conflict with others,* or *conflict with nature* to describe which type of conflict you will portray.
   _____

3. Brainstorm to improve on the plan for your story's conflict and outcome. On the lines below, describe the central problem or conflict, the triggering event, obstacles, the resolution or outcome, and as many plot details as you can. Use another sheet of paper if necessary.

   CENTRAL CONFLICT: _____
   _____
   _____
   _____

   TRIGGERING EVENT: _____
   _____
   _____
   _____

   OBSTACLES: _____
   _____
   _____
   _____
   _____
   _____

   RESOLUTION OR OUTCOME: _____
   _____
   _____
   _____

EXERCISE B Using the notes you have made from the previous exercises, you are now ready to write your story. Use the guidelines in your text for improving the plot, characterizations, and style of the story. When you have finished, revise and edit your draft.

Name _____   Date _____

CHAPTER 6   Writing a Play: Characters and Setting

EXERCISE A Read each of the following sample settings for a play. Think of a possible intriguing scenario that could happen in that setting. Make sure your ideas are dramatic and built around a possible conflict. Write your ideas on the blank lines.

1. An orphanage for teenagers in the 1950s

   _____
   _____
   _____

2. The announcer's box at a major league baseball game

   _____
   _____
   _____

3. A space station on the moon in 2022

   _____
   _____
   _____

4. A spooky house in the woods on Halloween night

   _____
   _____
   _____

5. The kitchen of New York City's most prestigious restaurant

   _____
   _____
   _____

EXERCISE B Choose one of the five scenarios you wrote about in Exercise A. Now create at least four unique characters who will carry out the action and conflict in the play. On a separate sheet of paper, write a character sketch for each. Be sure to answer questions such as *What does my character look like? What kind of personality does my character have? What patterns of speech does he or she have?* Include any other descriptions that will reveal aspects of your characters and assist the actors in your play.

Name _____ Date _____

CHAPTER 6 Writing a Play: Dialogue and Stage Directions

EXERCISE A Choose two of the characters you sketched in Exercise B on the previous page. Now imagine them in one of the following three scenarios. First, use the blank lines to freewrite about your ideas on what might happen between the characters in this situation. Then, on a separate sheet of paper, write a brief conversation between the characters that includes at least three individual speeches by each. Write only the dialogue, and do not worry about descriptions or stage directions. Try to reveal aspects of your characters' motivations and feelings through the lines of dialogue.

SCENARIO 1: Character 1 accidentally walks in on Character 2 and uncovers a secret

_____
_____
_____

SCENARIO 2: Character 1 and Character 2 eat breakfast together

_____
_____
_____

SCENARIO 3: Character 1 comes to the aid of Character 2, who does not feel well

_____
_____
_____

EXERCISE B Select one of the conversations you began with your sample characters. Now, on a separate sheet of paper, add stage directions to the scene, using details that you feel are necessary and that the audience would notice. Include props if they are necessary.

EXERCISE C Have your classmates read the scene you have just written. Hold a brief discussion about the elements of the scene, noting possible areas of improvement. Find areas where characters could become more realistic, where dialogue could become more natural-sounding, or where stage directions could be omitted or improved.

Name _____ Date _____

CHAPTER 6 Writing a Poem

> **EXERCISE A** Read the following list of prompts for poetry subjects. Then freewrite to list at least three possible events, scenes, and sensations that might be explored in a poem about each subject.

Example music
Events: a neighbor playing opera music; a morning radio broadcast; playing the trumpet
Scenes: my little sister's piano recital; an outdoor rock concert; children singing "Happy Birthday"
Sensations: the tingle in my ear at a soprano's voice; the taste of a clarinet reed; the feeling of fingers strumming a guitar

1. celebrations

    Events: _____
    Scenes: _____
    Sensations: _____

2. fears

    Events: _____
    Scenes: _____
    Sensations: _____

3. peaceful scenes

    Events: _____
    Scenes: _____
    Sensations: _____

4. famous people

    Events: _____
    Scenes: _____
    Sensations: _____

5. animals

    Events: _____
    Scenes: _____
    Sensations: _____

> **EXERCISE B** On a separate sheet of paper, write the first draft of a poem, either in rhyme or in free-verse form. Read your draft aloud to your classmates or friends.

Name _____ Date _____

CHAPTER 6 — Writing a Poem: Sound Language and Figurative Language

EXERCISE A For each sound device, list two possible examples to use in writing your poem.

1. **Onomatopoeia:** (the usage of words whose sounds suggest their meaning)
   _____
   _____

2. **Alliteration:** (repetition of a consonant sound at the beginning of a series of words)
   _____
   _____

3. **Consonance:** (repetition of a consonant sound or sounds, used with different vowel sounds, usually in the middle or at the end of words)
   _____
   _____

4. **Assonance:** (repetition of a vowel sound within words)
   _____
   _____

5. **Repetition:** (repetition of a word or phrase)
   _____
   _____

6. **Rhyme:** (repetition of accented syllables with the same vowel and consonant sounds)
   _____
   _____

continued

Chapter 6: Writing a Poem: Sound Language and Figurative Language *continued*

> **EXERCISE B** For each type of figurative language, list two possible examples to use in writing your poem. Use a separate sheet of paper for your work.

1. **Imagery** (use of concrete details to create a picture or appeal to senses other than sight)

2. **Simile** (comparison of unlike things, using the words *like* or *as*)

3. **Metaphor** (implied comparison of unlike things, without *like* or *as*)

4. **Personification** (use of human qualities attributed to something nonhuman)

5. **Hyperbole** (use of exaggeration or overstatement)

6. **Oxymoron** (use of opposite or contradictory terms)

7. **Symbol** (use of an object or action to stand for another)

Name _____   Date _____

CHAPTER 7 — Gathering Information

> **EXERCISE** Under each limited subject, write three supporting details that could serve as paragraph topics for the body of an essay.

Example **LIMITED SUBJECT:** coin collecting as a popular hobby

    I. *Collect coins as works of art*

    II. *Collect coins as an investment*

    III. *Acquire a complete set of a nation's coins or a set of a particular kind of coin*

1. **LIMITED SUBJECT:** changes in American eating habits since the time of Pilgrims

    I. _____

    II. _____

    III. _____

2. **LIMITED SUBJECT:** admirable traits in friends

    I. _____

    II. _____

    III. _____

3. **LIMITED SUBJECT:** clothing purposes

    I. _____

    II. _____

    III. _____

4. **LIMITED SUBJECT:** visiting museums broadens your knowledge of other cultures

    I. _____

    II. _____

    III. _____

5. **LIMITED SUBJECT:** advantages of being a teenager

    I. _____

    II. _____

    III. _____

CHAPTER 7 Organizing and Outlining

EXERCISE The following notes are on the subject of cacti. On the blank lines in the outline form below, write three categories into which you can group these notes. Then list each note under the proper heading.

1. Jam and syrup made from saguaro fruit
2. Water stored in thick, pulpy stem
3. Barrel cactus—shaped like water jug
4. Grow in hot, dry area like deserts
5. Tiny cacti used as home decorations
6. Grow spines instead of leaves
7. Fruit of prickly pear—a common treat along the Mexico/United States border
8. Night-blooming cereus
9. Saguaro—grow in Arizona and Mexico

I. _____
   A. _____
   B. _____
   C. _____

II. _____
   A. _____
   B. _____
   C. _____

III. _____
   A. _____
   B. _____
   C. _____

Name _____ Date _____

CHAPTER 7 Writing Informative Paragraphs

> **EXERCISE** On the blank line, indicate how each paragraph is developed. Choose from: *facts/examples, analysis of parts, comparison/contrast,* and *definition.*

_____ 1. Haiku-writing contests are popular in Japan. A haiku is a very short poem, having only seventeen syllables. The words are usually written in three lines of five, seven, and five syllables. In the few words, the haiku-writer sketches a picture of a thing or a happening. The writer does not tell what he or she feels or thinks. The reader must create a response to this picture. Thus the writer and the reader collaborate in a unique experience.

_____ 2. Badminton, which is derived from an ancient East Indian game, is quite similar to tennis. Tennis had been played in England for hundreds of years before British Army officers stationed in India brought the Indian game with them to England around 1870. Because the new game was first played there on the estate of the Duke of Beaufort, called "Badminton," it was given that name. As in tennis, two or four players use rackets to hit an object back and forth across a net. In badminton, however, a "bird" is used instead of a ball. The bird was originally a cork ball with a ring of feathers stuck into it. Unlike the tennis ball, it must not be allowed to hit the ground. The rackets are smaller and lighter than tennis rackets, and the bird flies much more slowly than the tennis ball.

_____ 3. Glass is made of a very common substance—sand. Actually, glassmakers use sand that is made from pulverized quartz, which is the most common of all minerals. In prehistoric times humans made such objects as knives from obsidian, a volcanic glass, and from rock crystal. In Egypt 4,000 years ago, glassmakers heated sand until it melted into a hot, syrupy liquid. Today glassmakers do the same, shaping the liquid by blowing, casting, drawing, pressing, cutting, or rolling. When this liquid cools, it becomes glass.

_____ 4. A computer system contains four parts. One part contains the keyboard and the built-in mechanism for conveying to the other three parts the messages you type. Another part contains the discs on which programs and data are recorded. A third part is the monitor, which looks like a television screen and which shows you what is going on in the first two parts as you press the various keys on the keyboard. Finally, the printer prints on paper whatever you and the other parts direct it to print. This four-part system has revolutionized our world.

CHAPTER 7 Drafting the Thesis Statement

EXERCISE Each of the following items includes the main topic and subtopics from an outline. On the blank lines, write a thesis statement that controls all of the main topics for each item.

1. I. Advantages to young people of living in Sulphur Springs, Arkansas
    A. Proximity to countryside for swimming, fishing, exploring
    B. Parks for concerts, baseball games, picnics

   II. Advantages to older people
    A. Many clubs and social groups
    B. Senior citizen center with facilities for teaching arts and crafts and serving tasty meals

THESIS STATEMENT
_____
_____
_____

2. I. Crops grown by colonial farmers in America
    A. Corn and wheat—principal crops in the eastern and middle colonies
    B. Rice and indigo—principal crops in the southern colonies

   II. Tools used for farming
    A. Use of hand tools, such as ax, hoe, scythe, sickle, and spade
    B. Use of homemade wooden plows with oxen

THESIS STATEMENT
_____
_____
_____

3. I. Preparation of a master city plan
    A. Consultation of city planner with experts such as architects, educators, and engineers
    B. Recommendations for use of city land

   II. Making the city plan work
    A. Gaining support of the public
    B. Gaining government authority to carry out the plan

THESIS STATEMENT
_____
_____
_____
_____

CHAPTER 7 Drafting the Introduction

> **EXERCISE** Read each introductory paragraph. Then, on the blank line, write *personal incident, background information,* or *attention-getting statement* to indicate how each paragraph begins.

_____ 1. Drivers along our major highways often hold their noses as they approach a car or van belching smelly fumes into the air. Today motor vehicle exhaust ranks as one of the nation's leading sources of air pollution. Each year cars release huge amounts of carbon monoxide, hydrocarbons, and nitrogen oxides into the air. It is the job of the Environmental Protection Agency to enforce standards that restrict the amount of pollution new cars can emit.

_____ 2. A major football team makes the headlines when its owners fire the manager or a popular halfback. Even bigger headlines occur when the owners sell an entire baseball team to a person in another city. Throughout the sports industry, as in most other industries, control is not exercised by the consumers (the fans) or the producers (the players) but by the owners.

_____ 3. I find that trying to read someone's signature on a letter or check is often difficult, if not impossible. Signatures, of course, are not the only difficulties. Many people write so poorly that reading script can be a very slow process. It seems that people don't mind their *p*'s and *q*'s and other letters as carefully as they might. Even in this age of computers, learning to write clearly and neatly is still a basic skill that every student should learn.

_____ 4. In the early days, people would open their newspapers to the comic strips for a good laugh. That is why comic strips were called "the funnies." Nowadays many comics describe events in the daily lives of family members, doctors, or police officers. Still others relate incidents in the lives of legendary people. Such comic strips, relating successions of incidents in the lives of the same characters, are not always comical. Nevertheless, many surveys indicate that comic strips are the most popular feature in newspapers.

Name _____ Date _____

CHAPTER 7 Body of a Composition

> **EXERCISE A** Read each thesis statement and then list two supporting ideas based on the main idea that could be developed into two paragraphs. Under each idea add two details you could use to develop that paragraph.

1. **THESIS STATEMENT:** The movies today can be exciting and entertaining, but often there is nothing better than watching a good black-and-white classic movie.

    I. _____
       a. _____
       b. _____
    II. _____
       a. _____
       b. _____

2. **THESIS STATEMENT:** It would benefit our cities if more people used public transportation when commuting.

    I. _____
       a. _____
       b. _____
    II. _____
       a. _____
       b. _____

3. **THESIS STATEMENT:** Although I certainly did not enjoy the time I spent being ill, it taught me a lesson about life.

    I. _____
       a. _____
       b. _____
    II. _____
       a. _____
       b. _____

> **EXERCISE B** Choose one of the three thesis statements from Exercise A. Now use the supporting ideas and details to freewrite on your ideas, developing a working body of an essay that explores your own ideas and opinions about the topic (you may want to make the thesis statement more specific or modify it to fit your own opinion). Use a separate sheet of paper and save your work.

Name _____ Date _____

CHAPTER 7 — Conclusion of a Composition

EXERCISE A Read the following concluding paragraphs. On the blank line, write the number of the clincher sentence(s) that does the better job. Then in one sentence write why you made your choice.

PARAGRAPH ONE:

The next time you take a long bike ride in the country, remember all the important safety reasons for wearing a helmet. And don't fret if you are still concerned with the strange and sometimes bulky look of some helmets.

---

1. There are many new models, after all, that are quite stylish and colorful. Imagine the heads that will turn when you speed past, wearing your new electric blue helmet, safely on your way to that beautiful, shady lake you've always wanted to visit!

2. The uncomfortable feeling you might get from wearing a helmet simply isn't as important as avoiding a terrible accident.

_____

_____

PARAGRAPH TWO:

Imagine my surprise when, last summer, I was walking through Central Park in the evening and saw a small family of raccoons. At that moment, I realized that even a city as large, loud, and bustling as New York City can have its own little haven for wild animals.

---

1. I walked out of the park, still thinking about this, and headed for the subway and went home.

2. The mother raccoon seemed to agree, as she waved her shiny black nose at me and scurried off with her pair of babies; it didn't matter that she was in a park in the middle of the city, because she was happy.

_____

_____

continued

Chapter 7: Conclusion of a Composition *continued*

EXERCISE B Write a clincher sentence, or sentences, that would work effectively for the following concluding paragraph.

> The directors of many of today's suspense and horror films, therefore, could learn a thing or two from Alfred Hitchcock. It's not hard to imagine these directors shuddering and shrieking at the nail-biting, nerve-jangling scenes from movies like *Psycho, The Birds, Vertigo,* and *North by Northwest.*

EXERCISE C Write a draft of the composition for which you developed supporting paragraphs and details in Exercise B on page 57. Add a strong conclusion. Then give your composition a title. Revise and edit your work carefully, and write a neat final copy. Then read and discuss your work with the rest of your class.

Name _____ Date _____

CHAPTER 7 Checking for Unity, Coherence, and Emphasis

EXERCISE Revise the following essay. You may make changes on this page.

1. Revise the thesis statement to control all the main topics.
2. Cross out any paragraphs that do not support the main topic, and delete any unnecessary words.
3. Add transitional words to help provide unity and coherence.

Exams are a part of every student's life, and every student wants to pass them with flying colors. This paper will be about my plan for passing exams. It has four main points. I have worked out a four-point program for passing exams, which I have used successfully.

It is too bad that students have to take so many exams. Many students don't do their best work on exams because they get so nervous.

Well, anyway, keeping up with class work is probably the most important way to prepare. Obviously, if you don't understand what is going on in the classroom, you won't understand the exam questions based on class work. Listening carefully and asking questions is what learning is all about. Taking notes on important points is a definite help, but be sure to review your notes before each class.

A second way to prepare for an exam is to keep up with the assignments. Do your homework. By doing your homework every day, you will quickly discover if you really understand what you have heard and read and whether you can apply that knowledge. If, for example, you have trouble with math homework, there is time to get help before the exam.

When the night before the exam arrives, check over the main points to be tested. Go over your notes again, and review summaries in your textbooks. If you have kept up with classroom work and assignments, you won't have to cram late into the night.

Arrive wide-awake and alert on the morning of the exam. A good night's sleep will help your brain to recall all the facts you have reviewed.

CHAPTER 8 Writing Persuasive Paragraphs

EXERCISE A Supply transitions for the following paragraph. Choose from *in addition, most important, furthermore,* and *in the first place*. Write your transitions on the blank lines below the paragraph.

I think that sunlight is the best direct source of energy. **(1)** _____, it does not pollute the environment, as coal, oil, and uranium do. **(2)** _____, it makes no noise, as furnaces and engines do. **(3)** _____, two of the most important advantages are that no country lacks sunlight and that it cannot be owned in the way coal, oil, and uranium are. **(4)** _____, the fact that sunlight costs nothing and never will cost anything means a great deal to most people. The supply of sunlight—unlike the stores of coal, oil, and uranium—will never give out.

1. _____
2. _____
3. _____
4. _____

EXERCISE B Follow the steps below to revise the persuasive paragraph. Make your changes on this page. Then copy the revised paragraph on a separate sheet of paper.

1. Arrange the sentences in order of importance (most to least).
2. Add transitional words.
3. Cross out emotionally charged words.

Going to our community college will enable me to get the education I want without endangering my financial status or leaving my friends. I will be able to keep my present friends. The most important consideration is that I want to be a dental hygienist, and all the skills I need are taught at our community college. I can live at home and commute to school rather than pay to live in a smelly, old dormitory. Also, I will be able to keep my present part-time job. Both living at home and keeping my job will help me solve my financial problems. You can see that my educational, financial, and social needs can be taken care of right here.

Name _____ Date _____

CHAPTER 8 Facts and Opinion; Reasoning

EXERCISE A On the blank line, tell whether each sentence expresses a fact or an opinion by writing *F* for fact or *O* for opinion. If you are in doubt, verify the information at the library or through a reliable authority.

Example __O__ A solar-heated home is best.

_____ 1. It is easier to float in salt water than in fresh water.

_____ 2. Swimming in salt water makes you feel better than swimming in freshwater.

_____ 3. There is too much violence on television.

_____ 4. Golf is a less physically demanding game than tennis.

_____ 5. The number of hours of sunlight in July was twice that in January.

_____ 6. Mathematics is the hardest subject of all.

_____ 7. Viewing Channel 13 between 8:00 and 11:00 last night, I counted 30 acts of violence.

_____ 8. My lowest grade this year was in mathematics.

_____ 9. A recent poll showed that the average age of golfers was eleven years higher than the average age of tennis players.

_____ 10. Winter is the worst season of the year.

EXERCISE B Write one fact that could be used to back up each opinion below. Use references like encyclopedias and almanacs.

Example The fishing in Adirondack lakes is getting worse.
Fish and Game Department studies say that there were fewer bass in Blue Mountain Lake last year than there were ten years ago.

1. Cities were noisier 100 years ago than they are today.
   _____

2. Basketball games are more exciting than football games.
   _____

3. English is a more nearly international language than French.
   _____

4. Exercise is good for you.
   _____

5. More United States citizens should vote in national elections.
   _____

Name _____ Date _____

CHAPTER 8 Recognizing Propaganda

EXERCISE A Label each statement *F* for fact or *O* for opinion.

Example Hank Aaron is in the National Baseball Hall of Fame.   F

1. Babe Ruth and Joe DiMaggio played for the New York Yankees. _____
2. Eating Krunchies will make you a champion ballplayer. _____
3. An actress's hairdresser has a great influence on her career. _____
4. In the year 2000, January 1 fell on a Saturday. _____
5. Lincoln was fifty-two when he became president. _____
6. Lincoln was our greatest president. _____
7. Establishing colonies on Mars would be a waste of talent and money. _____
8. Newspaper reports of events are not always accurate. _____
9. School cafeteria food is awful. _____
10. I don't like school cafeteria food. _____

EXERCISE B Label each statement *B* for bandwagon, *T* for testimonial, or *U* for unproved generalization.

Example Miss America uses Oralight to keep her winning smile.   T

1. Give your kids EduGame, the new computer program that guarantees high grades. _____
2. Everybody who is anybody is wearing Antelope jeans. _____
3. The star of *Fancy Dancing* owes her success in that role to her training in the ancient Asian art of self-defense. _____
4. "Just-say-Da," a four-tape Russian language lesson, will have you chatting with Boris in just six weeks. _____
5. In Hollywood they are all using Wall Climber to keep themselves slender while they eat all the food they wish. _____

EXERCISE C Using your imagination, write a bandwagon appeal or a testimonial. Read it aloud to your classmates to see if they can tell which approach you used.

Name _____ Date _____

CHAPTER 8 Choosing a Subject; Developing a Thesis Statement

EXERCISE A On a separate sheet of paper, use brainstorming or freewriting techniques to complete each of the following statements.

1. The things I enjoy most about the city are . . .

2. The problems that concern me about the city are . . .

3. The issues that concern my friends and neighbors are . . .

4. Some aspects of city life I would like to change are . . .

5. If the city had more money to spend, I would suggest spending it on . . .

EXERCISE B Indicate whether each statement is suitable or unsuitable for a persuasive essay. Then write *S* for suitable or *U* for unsuitable on the blank line.

Example __S__ On weekends traffic should be banned from streets in our city parks.

_____ 1. I am horrified by the amount of pushing and shoving on city buses.

_____ 2. The number of city bus routes has risen from 15 to 19.

_____ 3. One way to keep traffic moving is to create more one-way streets.

_____ 4. The Highway Department should spend additional funds to repave many downtown streets.

_____ 5. Those of us who use city buses should learn to be more polite to each other.

EXERCISE C Choose one of your ideas from Exercise A above, and then write a one-sentence thesis statement.

_____

_____

_____

Name _____ Date _____

CHAPTER 8 Organizing an Argument

EXERCISE A Below each thesis statement are three supporting ideas. Number these items in order of least important (1) to most important (3). Be ready to justify your answers.

1. Young people should watch less television.

    _____ They are likely to eat too many unhealthy snacks.

    _____ They may watch unrewarding programs.

    _____ They take time from more active pursuits with friends and potential friends.

2. The United States should not spend the money to send people to Mars.

    _____ The cost would be tremendous.

    _____ Other worthwhile programs need funds that would be used for a Mars program.

    _____ We can see through our telescopes what Mars is like.

3. A feeling of self-worth is an important asset.

    _____ It helps in making and keeping friends and getting and keeping a good job.

    _____ It helps in getting up and speaking in front of a group.

    _____ It makes a person feel happier about his/her life in general.

4. Cats should be kept on leashes, just as dogs are.

    _____ Cats sometimes wander off.

    _____ Cats sometimes destroy plants or animals in neighbors' yards.

    _____ Cats can be stolen or hit by passing cars.

EXERCISE B Using the thesis statement you developed in Exercise C on page 64, develop arguments and organize your ideas into a short outline. Then prepare a draft of your essay.

Name _____   Date _____

CHAPTER 9 Responding from Personal Experience

EXERCISE Choose a piece of literature you have read that particularly appealed to you and answer the following questions about it.

Title _____

Author _____

1. Which character did you identify with most closely? Why?
   _____
   _____
   _____

2. Did your feelings about the character remain the same or change as you read further? Why?
   _____
   _____
   _____

3. Which character reminded you of someone you know? Why?
   _____
   _____
   _____

4. What situations made you think of situations in you own life? How were the situations alike or different from your own experience?
   _____
   _____
   _____

5. What feelings did the work evoke in you?
   _____
   _____
   _____

Name _____ Date _____

CHAPTER 9 Responding from Literary Knowledge

EXERCISE Read the following poem by Robert Frost and answer the questions that follow.

> **Stopping by Woods on a Snowy Evening**
>
> Whose woods these are I think I know.
> His house is in the village though;
> He will not see me stopping here
> To watch his woods fill up with snow.
>
> My little horse must think it queer
> To stop without a farmhouse near
> Between the woods and frozen lake
> The darkest evening of the year.
>
> He gives his harness bells a shake
> To ask if there is some mistake.
> The only other sound's the sweep
> Of easy wind and downy flake.
>
> The woods are lovely, dark and deep.
> But I have promises to keep,
> And miles to go before I sleep,
> And miles to go before I sleep.
> —*Robert Frost*

1. How would you describe the persona of the poem?

   _____
   _____

2. How do the meter and rhyme scheme of the poem add to your image of the person?

   _____
   _____
   _____

continued

Name _____ Date _____

Chapter 9: Responding from Literary Knowledge *continued*

3. How does the horse's shaking his harness bells contribute symbolically to the theme?
   _____
   _____

4. What feeling, theme, or message does the poem express?
   _____

5. Does the last line create a different meaning in you from the identical preceding line?
   _____

6. How does "easy wind" contribute to the meaning you get from the poem?
   _____

CHAPTER 9 Evaluating a Literary Work

EXERCISE Carefully read Lillian Morrison's poem "The Women's 400 Meters" to prepare for a critical essay you will write about the poet's use of figurative language. Then answer the questions that follow the poem. Use another sheet of paper if necessary.

The Women's 400 Meters

Skittish,
they flex knees, drum heels and
shiver at the starting line

waiting for the gun
to pour them over the stretch
like a breaking wave.

Bang! they're off
careening down the lanes,
each chased by her own bright tiger.

—Lillian Morrison

1. Do you like the poem? Why or why not?
   _____

2. What experiences of your own does the poem remind you of?
   _____
   _____
   _____

3. How does the imagery of the poem support the tenseness of the scene?
   _____
   _____

continued

Chapter 9: Evaluating a Literary Work *continued*

4. What are the runners compared to in the second stanza? What does this comparison add to the description of the runners?

   _____

   _____

   _____

5. What does the metaphor of the tiger stand for? What is it really that makes the runners go as fast as they can? What does this metaphor contribute to the poem's theme?

   _____

   _____

   _____

CHAPTER 9 — Developing a Thesis; Evidence; Outlining

EXERCISE A What exactly would you like to say about "The Women's 400 Meters"? Write some ideas here. Then write a working thesis statement.

_____
_____
_____
_____
_____
_____
_____
_____

THESIS STATEMENT: _____
_____
_____

EXERCISE B Complete the following activities to gather your evidence and write an outline.

1. Look for words, phrases, and lines in the poem that support your thesis statement. You might note, for instance, that both the simile of the wave and the metaphor of the tiger suggest the speed and power of the runners. Write each detail and what it means or adds to the poem on a note card or slip of paper.

2. Think of two main points you can make to support your thesis. On a separate sheet of paper, write these down as the main points (Roman numerals) in an outline.

3. Use the details from your note cards as supporting points (capital letters) in the outline.

Name _____ Date _____

CHAPTER 9 Drafting; Using Quotations; Revising

EXERCISE A Complete the following activities to draft your essay.

1. Draft an introduction that tells the name of the poem and the poet and includes your thesis statement.

2. Draft the body, using your outline as a guide. Use present tense verbs to tell what the poem says.

3. Draft a conclusion that sums up your thesis and the details that support it.

4. Add a title that tells what your essay is about.

EXERCISE B Use these questions to guide your revising. Freewrite your answers on the lines provided.

1. Is my thesis clearly stated?
   _____
   _____

2. Is my thesis supported with enough details or quotations from the poem?
   _____
   _____
   _____

3. Do the details show what I say they show?
   _____
   _____

4. Do all of my points stick to the thesis? Is the essay unified?
   _____
   _____
   _____

5. Do I use transitions to show how ideas are related?
   _____
   _____

6. Does my conclusion sum up my thesis and my evidence?
   _____
   _____
   _____

Name _____ Date _____

CHAPTER 10 Recognizing Main Ideas

> **EXERCISE** On the blank lines, write the main idea of each paragraph. If the main idea is stated directly, copy it. If it is implied, write a sentence of your own that expresses the main idea.

1. Since your skeleton supports you, you should give your skeleton good support. Your bones are living, changing parts of your body. As you grow up, they have to grow longer and stronger. Their principal building material is calcium. Bones need plenty of calcium as you are growing up, and they continue to need calcium as long as you live. If you want to be able to bowl or play tennis when you are eighty, keep taking calcium. Don't let your skeleton become weak and frail.

   _____

   _____

2. In thousands of communities across the United States, there are volunteer rescue squads. These squads are composed of men and women who give their time and energy to aid people in distress. If a child is lost, the rescue squad will turn out to search the neighborhood. If someone has an automobile accident, the squad will promptly give first aid, help start the car again, or haul it off the road. For all these invaluable services, they will charge nothing.

   _____

   _____

3. In any burglar alarm system, there are three main elements—the sensors, the master control, and the alarm. The sensors are located by windows and doors and also within rooms. The sensors are wired (or connected by radio) to the master control unit, which is the "brain" of the system. When something affects the sensors, they communicate this fact to the "brain," whereupon the "brain" sends a message to the alarm. The alarm sounds a warning, a frightening scream, which says to the burglar, "You'd better get out of here."

   _____

   _____

4. What every used-car buyer needs is a good guarantee from a reliable dealer. Wisconsin has perhaps the best law for protecting used-car purchasers. Every dealer has to examine every car according to a state-supplied checklist. On this list the dealer must note what is found and what has been done about any defect. If the user's experience shows that the dealer did not make a correct report, the dealer is compelled by law to make an adjustment satisfactory to the buyer.

   _____

   _____

Name _____ Date _____

CHAPTER 10 Condensing

EXERCISE On the blank lines, condense each paragraph to no more than two sentences.

1. Some people like to keep pigeons. I have often wondered why. They don't eat them—though our ancestors did. Many homes in England, 300 or 400 years old, had holes in outside walls in which pigeons lived. The birds were a convenient source of food. Pigeon fanciers today don't even eat the eggs and don't appear to benefit in any other way. I wonder if these people enjoy watching their pets maneuver through the sky. Maybe they enjoy having creatures around that are dependent on them for food and shelter. Whatever the reward, they seem willing to pay in time and money to support their feathered friends.

   _____

   _____

2. Sea oats are a kind of grass that grows on the beaches from the Chesapeake Bay to the Caribbean Sea. Along the tops of the dunes, they grow about four feet high and bend gracefully under the pressure of the winds and of the birds that feed on their seeds. They look fragile, but they are tough enough to withstand the battering of winds and salt spray from ocean waves. In fact, they are so strong that they protect the sand dunes, which hold the ocean back and keep it from flooding the lowlands. Their tap roots go down ten feet or more, and their maze of underground stems extends outward for a radius of six feet. People who pick sea oats for decorations kill the plants. If the sea oats perish, the dunes will be swept away.

   _____

   _____

3. People in different countries eat somewhat different foods. Europeans and Americans eat bread made of wheat flour and raised by yeast. Mexicans prefer tortillas, a flat bread made of ground corn. Tibetans drink yak milk; Lapplanders drink reindeer milk; Iranians drink goat milk. Many Americans would not enjoy being served snails, grasshoppers, or turtles' eggs, but these are considered delicacies in some countries. We are all likely to prefer the foods popular in our own country.

   _____

   _____

4. A thousand years ago, Iceland had many forests and little ice. Many Norse people emigrated to Iceland where they proceeded to cut down most of the trees. Their only fuel was wood. They brought sheep with them, and the sheep also destroyed trees by eating the bark. Even today Icelanders depend on sheep for most of their income. Now they protect their few forests with fences, and they are planting trees by the thousands. They hope to recreate an Iceland of many forests and little ice.

   _____

   _____

CHAPTER 10 Paraphrasing

EXERCISE A Rewrite each group of sentences below in your own words. Replace words in the originals with synonyms, and vary the structures of the original sentences.

1. The kinds of oils, wicks, and holders that were used changed at different times and in different societies. But the principle of the lamp remained basically the same for centuries.

2. The American colonist who lacked a starter flame or glowing embers was sometimes confronted by a serious problem: how to light the lamp.

3. On darker days the capricious tinderbox, with its flint and steel, was needed.

4. Covered ember scoops or pierced tin lanterns served as carriers for the borrowed flames.

EXERCISE B Rewrite the three sentences of this paragraph in your own words, paraphrasing to change sentence structure and word choice. Use a separate sheet of paper for your work.

> The city hall of Lambertville was built in 1853 and overseen by John Washington Pemberly, a man famous in the state for his successful Lambertville printing business. Records show that a time capsule was buried under the stone steps of the city hall, and directions in these records state that the capsule cannot be unearthed until 2053. In the past 150 years, Lambertville has seen five tornadoes and season after season of terrible weather, but it seems that the city hall, in some form or other, might still be standing in 50 more years.

Name _____ Date _____

CHAPTER 11   Evaluating Sources

EXERCISE Assume that you are doing research on the subject of buying the best bicycle. You have located the sources below, but each has a weakness. On the blank line, identify the weakness of each source using the following phrases:

  probably outdated
  probably biased
  lacks strong author credentials
  does not relate to subject

1. "How to Find Best Buys in Used Bicycles," an article in *Mechanix Illustrated*, published in 1974, written by M. Dowd, president of a bicycle club.

   _____

2. "The Best Bicycle for You," an article in a Streamline Bicycle Company booklet, published in 2008, written by C. Clark, an officer of the company.

   _____

3. "Evaluating Motorbikes," an article in *Science Today*, published in 2007, written by G. Holden, staff writer.

   _____

4. "Bicycle Trips," an article on the Women at Work Web site, posted in May 2008.

   _____

5. "Buying a Used Bicycle," an article in *Women on the Job*, published in 1999, written by S. Hall, a freelance writer on food and fashion.

   _____

6. "Guide to Bicycle Shopping," an article in *Business Week*, published in 1998, written by an unnamed staff writer.

   _____

7. *The Mechanics of the Bicycle Clutch*, published in 2006, a book by F. Filson, a professor of mechanical engineering.

   _____

8. "New Equipment for Better Biking," an article in *Sports Illustrated*, published in 1989, written by B. McDermitt, staff writer.

   _____

CHAPTER 11 Using the Library or Media Center

EXERCISE A On the blank line, write the letter under which you would find each of the following titles on the fiction or biography shelves in a library.

1. *Thomas Jefferson* by Fawn Brodie _____

2. *Transformations* by Anne Sexton _____

3. *The Whistling Song* by Stephen Beachy _____

4. *The Boxcar Children* by Gertrude Chandler Warner _____

5. *The Story of My Life* by Helen Keller _____

EXERCISE B Match a call number from the list to each of the titles below and write it on the blank line. Use this guide to the Dewey Decimal System to help you.

Call Numbers	Main Subject Area in the Dewey Decimal System
016.33	000–099 General Works (reference books)
109	100–199 Philosophy
201	200–299 Religion
370.1	300–399 Social Science (law, education, economics)
422	400–499 Language
507.6	500–599 Science (mathematics, biology, chemistry)
609.73	600–699 Technology (medicine, inventions)
792	700–799 Fine Arts (painting, music, theater)
809	800–899 Literature
901	900–999 History (biography, geography, travel)

1. *Science Brain-Twisters, Paradoxes, and Fallacies* _____

2. *The Families of Words* _____

3. *Life in the Theater* _____

4. *The Story of Philosophy* _____

5. *Democracy and Education* _____

6. *Technology in America* _____

7. *The Lessons of History* _____

8. *The Encyclopedia of Business Information Sources* _____

9. *What Is Religion?* _____

10. *The Ironic Vision in Modern Literature* _____

CHAPTER 11 Using Print and Non-Print Reference Materials

EXERCISE A Using the following list of library resources, select the best resource for finding the answer to each question. Write your choice on the line provided.

online card catalog
specialized encyclopedia
specialized dictionary
atlas
Readers' Guide

general encyclopedia
biographical reference
index
almanac
vertical file

Example When was Mickey Mantle inducted into the Baseball Hall of Fame? _almanac_

1. What are two synonyms for the word *infer*? _____
2. In what year was Willa Cather born? _____
3. What are the names of the Great Lakes? _____
4. Who wrote the poem "Trees"? _____
5. Who won the Pulitzer Prize for fiction in 1953? _____
6. What recent articles have been published on recycling trash? _____
7. What are the entrance requirements for the University of Texas? _____
8. How many books by Gerald Durrell does your library have? _____
9. Which artist is famous for making mobiles? _____
10. What are the principal crops of Iowa? _____
11. What is the name of a mountain range in Mexico? _____
12. What is the population of the largest county in the United States? _____
13. Who has written a recent article on fishing? _____
14. What are the most important highlights of Senator Nunn's life? _____
15. What is the title of a pamphlet on lifesaving? _____

continued

Chapter 11: Using Print and Non-Print Reference Materials *continued*

> **EXERCISE B** Using the resources in your library, find answers to the first five questions in Exercise A.

1. _____
2. _____
3. _____
4. _____
5. _____

Name _____ Date _____

CHAPTER 11 Taking Notes and Summarizing

EXERCISE Assume that you are participating in a history class presentation covering the years of the Kennedy administration. You have just read the following excerpt and are ready to take notes. On the blank lines below, identify the aspect of the subject being discussed. Then summarize the main points in your own words. Include a good direct quotation.

> In 1960, under President John F. Kennedy, the United States government founded the Peace Corps. In his inaugural address, Kennedy had said, "Ask not what your country can do for you. Rather, ask what you can do for your country." With these words was born the motivating idea behind the Peace Corps: to work in developing nations so that these nations and the United States could better understand one another. In this way the Peace Corps workers would be serving the United States and third-world countries.
>
> A Peace Corps volunteer must be at least 18 years old, possess American citizenship, and have useful skills. Volunteers come from many backgrounds, and their various skills meet the needs of many countries. For example, if the government of a developing nation needs to improve its sanitary conditions, the Peace Corps will be able to send trained volunteers who are experienced in public health.
>
> After joining the Peace Corps, volunteers go through a training program in which they learn to adapt their skills to the job they have been assigned. They also learn about the country they will work in. If the volunteers don't know the language of the country, they will be given language instruction. Many of the early volunteers got so much out of their experiences that, in 1964, the United States set up a similar program to serve Americans. This program was called VISTA, an acronym for Volunteers in Service to America.
>
> Both VISTA and the Peace Corps continue to operate, fulfilling President Kennedy's call for active engagement in dealing with the world's problems.

1. **ASPECT OF SUBJECT:**
   _____
   _____

2. **DIRECT QUOTATION:**
   _____
   _____
   _____

3. **MAIN POINTS SUMMARIZED:**
   _____
   _____
   _____

Name _____ Date _____

CHAPTER 12 — Writing a Working Thesis Statement; Organizing Notes

> **EXERCISE** On the lines below, write the three main categories into which the following pieces of information can be grouped. Next to each category, list the letters of the items that fall under each heading. Then write a working thesis statement for a research paper on the subject.

Subject: Special uses of television

a. Television cameras are placed in operating rooms.

b. Guards watch prisoners on closed-circuit television sets.

c. Open-circuit broadcasts are shown in some schools.

d. School-wide viewing of special events, such as presidential inaugurations, is possible through television.

e. Close-up pictures of actual operations are watched by medical students.

f. Specially prepared lessons are received in classrooms.

g. Prison officials observe visitors to prisons on television sets.

h. New employees are instructed and familiarized with hospital facilities.

Category 1: _____
Category 2: _____
Category 3: _____
WORKING THESIS STATEMENT: _____
_____

continued

Name _____ Date _____

Chapter 12: Writing a Working Thesis Statement; Organizing Notes *continued*

Subject: Underwater diving

   a. *Scuba* stands for "self-contained underwater breathing apparatus."

   b. Skin divers may use no equipment at all.

   c. Surface-supplied divers wear waterproof suits and helmets.

   d. Skin divers often use face masks, snorkels, and flippers.

   e. Surface-supplied divers get air or breathing gas through a hose connected to air pumps on a boat.

   f. Scuba divers wear metal tanks that hold compressed air.

   g. A scuba diver breathes air from a tank, and the exhaled air is released into the water.

Category 1: _____

Category 2: _____

Category 3: _____

WORKING THESIS STATEMENT: _____

_____

CHAPTER 12 Outlining

EXERCISE On the blank lines, complete the outline below. Use the following unsorted entries.

In other countries	Finishing fabric	Making yarn
Polyester	Natural fibers	Textile industry
Wool	Twill weave	Knitted

I. Sources of textile fibers
   A. _Natural fibers_
      1. Silk
      2. _Wool_
      3. Cotton
   B. Synthetic fibers
      1. Rayon
      2. Nylon
      3. _Polyester_

II. Kinds of fabrics
   A. Woven
      1. Plain weave
      2. _Twill weave_
   B. _Knitted_
   C. Other fabrics

III. Production of fabrics
   A. Designing
   B. _Making yarn_
   C. Making fabric
   D. _Finishing fabric_

IV. Textile industry
   A. In the United States
   B. In Canada
   C. _In other countries_

Name _____ Date _____

CHAPTER 12 — Lists of Works Cited

EXERCISE Use the works cited models below to write the information about each source in correct form.

ENCYCLOPEDIA: Barnes, Josiah, ed. The Columbia Encyclopedia. Sixth ed. New York: Columbia University Press, 2009. http://www.encyclopedia.com/doc/1E1-computer.html (accessed July 21, 2009).

BOOK: Carr, Nicholas. The Big Switch: Rewiring the World, from Edison to Google. New York: W. W. Norton & Co., 2008.

MAGAZINE ARTICLE: George, Aleta. "Booting Up a Computer Pioneer's 200-Year-Old Design." Smithsonian, April 2, 2009.

JOURNAL ARTICLE: Peck, Sharon M. "Not on the Same Page but Working Together." The Reading Teacher 63, no. 5 (February 2010): 394–403.

1. **SOURCE:** The Reading Teacher 62, no. 4 "Vocabulary Instruction." pages 333–336. March 2009. Sam Sebastian

   _____

   _____

2. **SOURCE:** Cyber Crime, Andrew Grant-Adamson, Mason Crest Publishers New York, 2003.

   _____

   _____

3. **SOURCE:** Tiffany Sharples, June 9, 2009, Time, "Another Computer Hazard: Dropping One on Your Foot."

   _____

   _____

4. **SOURCE:** Microsoft Encarta Online Encyclopedia, "Central Processing Unit," 2009, http://encarta.msn.com, accessed on today's date, third edition. Microsoft, Redmond

   _____

   _____

5. **SOURCE:** Personal Computing Demystified, page 215, Larry E. Long, 2004, McGraw-Hill, New York

   _____

   _____